Living Faith

A Statement of Christian Belief

Wood Lake Books Inc.
Winfield, B.C.

Published for
The Presbyterian Church in Canada
by
Wood Lake Books Inc.
Box 700,
Winfield, B.C.
V0H 2C0

ISBN 0-919599-20-6

INTRODUCTION

In every generation the church needs to confess its faith anew. That confession must at one and the same time be the ancient faith of the church and yet spoken into the mood and questions of its own time. LIVING FAITH endeavours to do that. This *Statement of Christian Belief* was prepared under the direction of the Committee on Church Doctrine of The Presbyterian Church in Canada. It has been received by the General Assembly of that Church and commended as an acceptable statement and as useful in both worship and study.

While arising out of the Canadian Presbyterian experience, it is hoped that the statement speaks to a much wider circle than one denomination, and to people outside the church. Here, perhaps for the first time, a confessional statement recognizes doubt, and in the midst of its ringing affirmation of Christian truth acknowledges the difficulties of belief and the ambiguities of the life of faith.

In writing this document the authors have tried to be in contact with people where they are today. Thus the statement speaks not only of God's work in Christ, but also of sex, war, the economy, the family, and justice. We believe that all this is fitting in a faith which has as its central affirmation the great truth that "God was in Christ reconciling the world unto himself." The living God became the person of Christ and walked in our midst in a world that to an astonishing extent shared many of the same problems we do now. If God could get involved with the grim fabric of life, then so can God's church! So too, must the faith we confess.

The inspiration for the style and general outline of LIVING FAITH comes from *A Declaration of Faith* of The Presbyterian Church in the United States. Some use has also been made of modern statements such as *The Confession of 1967* of The United Presbyterian Church in the U.S.A. and others listed in the notes. We are grateful for permission to use these statements. The committee responsible for LIVING FAITH always had in mind the great Reformed Confessions such as the *Westminster Confession,* the *Scots Confession* and the *Heidelberg Catechism.* In the end the statement is our own, reflecting our own needs and experiences.

In 1536 George Wishart, the first teacher of the Scottish Reformation, translated a Confession of Faith. Part of his introduction to that statement is appropriate today: "It is not our mind to prescribe a certain rule of the faith to all churches, for we know no other rule of faith but the Holy Scriptures; and therefore we are well contented with those who agree with these things, although they use another manner of speaking. It was our pleasure to use these words at the present time, that we might declare our opinion in our religion and worshipping of God. The truth will have the upper hand."

LIVING FAITH
A STATEMENT OF CHRISTIAN BELIEF

CHAPTER ONE

God

1.1   There is one true God
whom to know is life eternal,
whom to serve is joy and peace.
God has created all that is.
The whole universe testifies
to the majesty and power of its Maker.

1.2   God has come to us.
The Lord spoke to the people of Israel
and entered into covenant with them.
From Israel came Jesus Christ,
the Son of God,
bringing salvation through a new covenant
entered by faith.
The Lord continues to come to us by the Holy Spirit,
God present in the world,
and Guide to the church, the new Israel.

1.3   The church upholds and defends the truth
given to the apostles
and recorded in the Scriptures.
The Old and New Testaments
witness to God's mighty acts.
They reveal the Creator's holy love,
and lead us to Jesus Christ.

1.4   The creeds of the early church
preserve the faith of the apostles
who first preached the Gospel of Christ.
We receive them as a legacy
in which the true interpretation of the Scriptures
is protected.

1.5   Therefore, with the one church universal
we believe in one God, eternal Trinity,
Father, Son and Holy Spirit,
three in one,
one in three,
equal in power and glory.
God is the Father to whom we come,

the Son through whom we come,
the Spirit by whom we come.

1.6   We worship almighty God, the source of all life.
With thanks we acknowledge
God's wisdom, power, faithfulness, and love.
Glory be to the Father, and to the Son,
and to the Holy Spirit,
as it was in the beginning, is now,
and ever shall be!

CHAPTER TWO

2.1   God Creates and Rules

2.1.1   The living God is Lord,
Creator of all, Sustainer and Ruler of the universe.
In the seasons and the harvests,
in the rise and fall of nations,
God's goodness and judgement are present.
All events in this world
are under the sovereign care of the eternal God.

2.1.2   We hold in reverence the whole creation
as the theatre of God's glory and action.
God rules the lives of individuals and nations
yet does not negate our freedom and responsibility.
Ever at work in the world and in our lives
God directs all things towards fulfilment in Christ.

2.1.3   We affirm God's righteous and loving purpose
even in a world where evil abounds.
This purpose is uniquely disclosed in Jesus Christ.
In him we see the greatest paradox of life:
the mighty God chose to come into this world in weakness.
In Christ, God entered most deeply into our suffering.

2.1.4   We cannot fully comprehend
nor is it our task to justify
God's rule of the world.
We experience evil in the midst of life.
Yet evil cannot ultimately prevail,
for it is against God's will.

The resurrection of Christ
and the new life he gives us
are assurance of his ultimate triumph.

2.2 Our Creation

2.2.1   The mystery of human existence
is that we belong to God
and have been made in the divine image.
In God we live and move and have our being.
Therefore, we know ourselves
only when we know God.
Our lives must reflect
the Creator's love and purpose for all creation.
We acknowledge God as Creator and Lord.

2.2.2   We have been made male and female
for our mutual help, comfort and joy.
Our creation as sexual beings
is God's loving purpose for us.
We are dependent on each other and
as men and women, need one another in all of life.

2.3 Our Calling

2.3.1   We are called to work out the meaning of our own lives
and to find our true vocation
in the love and service of God.

2.3.2   We serve and love God
by the service and love of creation
especially the care of the needy.
Every kind of work
that is honest and serves others
is a vocation from the Lord.

2.3.3   Calling means the necessity
to deny selfish ambition and desire
in order to minister to others.
In God's service true freedom is to be found.

2.4 Our Care for the World

2.4.1   Though life is a gift from God,
human life depends on the created world.

Our care for the world must reflect God's care.
We are not owners, but stewards of God's good earth.
Concerned with the well-being of all of life
we welcome the truths and insights
of all human skill and science
about the world and the universe.

2.4.2   Our stewardship calls us
to explore ways of love and justice
in respecting God's creation
and in seeking its responsible use
for the common good.

2.5   **Sin Separates Us from God**

2.5.1   We confess that we are sinners.
We do not care for the world as we should.
We do not fulfil our calling to serve God.
Our lives do not reflect the Creator's love.
Our failure is sin,
a rebellion against God,
an insistence that we be god in our own lives.

2.5.2   God has given us the law
to show us how to live.
Yet we are unable to keep the Ten Commandments,
and we do not love God without reserve
nor our neighbour as ourselves.
Above all, our sin is exposed
by the perfect life of Christ.

2.5.3   Sin alienates us from God.
It offends the holiness of God,
separates us from our Lord,
and leads to spiritual death.
It mars the divine image in us
and infects our relationship with others
and with ourselves.

2.5.4   Sin is a power present
in every human life, even at birth.
It issues in such sins as
pride asserting itself against God,
indifference towards God and neighbour,

untruthfulness, greed, lust, laziness,
gluttony, envy, and selfish anger.

2.5.5   We cannot escape our sin,
nor the sin of the world.

2.5.6   Because we are sinful
the societies we live in are sinful.
There are no exceptions:
every system is flawed.
We are part of the evil of the world,
of its violence, neglect, injustice.

2.5.7   All people fall short of God's standards
and need salvation.
God's way to salvation
has been revealed in Jesus Christ.
Through the death and resurrection of Christ
our sins are forgiven.
Salvation means life, forgiveness, healing, wholeness.
It comes from God's grace
received through faith in Christ alone.

2.5.8   Thanks be to God!

CHAPTER THREE    God in Christ

3.1   Jesus Christ and Israel

3.1.1   To the world in its rebellion and alienation
God promised blessing and restoration.
The Lord chose Abraham and his descendants
and through a covenant with them
destined them to be bearers of that promise to all people.

3.1.2   The Old Testament records
God's message and mighty acts.
It speaks of God's grace and judgement.
It declares God's promise
and points to the One to come.

3.1.3   From Israel came the Messiah;
in Jesus of Nazareth God kept the promise of salvation.

We understand his coming in the light of the Old Testament.
Born of the seed of David, he lived a Jew among Jews.
Child of an Israelite woman, he fulfilled God's promise
that Israel would be a light to the nations.
In Christ God came to dispel the world's darkness.

3.2 **Jesus Christ: Truly God**

3.2.1 God became man
and dwelt among us.
In silence we ponder,
in awe we confess
this amazing truth.
Conceived by the Holy Spirit,
born of the Virgin Mary,
the eternal Son of God
humbled himself
to be one with us.
To Israel and to the world
came God in Christ.

3.2.2 To call Jesus Christ the Son of God
is to say that he is
God of God, Light of Light
begotten, not made.
To see Jesus is to see God incarnate.
To know the Son is to know the Father.

3.2.3 God's nature is expressed in Jesus,
the very Word of God.
Through him were all things made.
His life is the light of the world.

3.2.4 Jesus Christ is Lord.
He is one with the Father
and the Holy Spirit.

3.3 **Jesus Christ: Truly Human**

3.3.1 Jesus was truly human.
Tried and tested as we are,
yet without sin,
he experienced the depths of life.
Jesus understands us.
He felt the joy of friendship,

the pain of rejection,
and died a human death.
He trusted the Father completely
and lived in the Holy Spirit.
Neither temptation nor threat
prevented him from loving God
and his neighbour as himself.
He showed us what it means
to be a child of God.

3.4 **Jesus is Saviour**

3.4.1 Jesus is the Mediator
through whom God has come to us
and through whom we come to God.

3.4.2 Christ died for our sins.
The innocent one bore our condemnation on the cross.
He suffered and was put to death
for the sin of the world.

3.4.3 God's reconciling act in Jesus Christ is a mystery
which the Scriptures describe as
the sacrifice of a lamb,
a shepherd's life given for his sheep,
atonement by a priest.
It is also the innocent dying for the guilty,
the ransom of a slave,
payment of a debt,
and victory over the powers of evil.
Such expressions interpret the love of God
revealing the gravity, cost, and sure achievement
of our Lord's work.
Yet that love we cannot fully explain.
God's grace, received by faith alone,
pardons and justifies,
redeems and reconciles us.

3.5 **Jesus is Lord**

3.5.1 Jesus suffered, died, and was buried,
but God raised him from the dead.
Risen and ascended,
he is alive now, the living Lord.

3.5.2   His resurrection means that our faith is not empty,
that final victory is assured over all evil powers
which destroy and deform life,
and that death, the last enemy, is conquered.

3.5.3   The forces of the evil one still wage war against us.
The destructive powers are still present.
But their end is not in doubt.
We await the full revelation of our Lord's triumph.

3.5.4   We worship our ascended Lord.
Reigning in glory and power
he is our High Priest and Advocate
interceding before the Father on our behalf.
Through him we offer our sacrifice of praise,
with prayer for all to the Father.

3.5.5.   Thanks be to God who gives us the victory
through Jesus Christ our Lord!

3.6   Salvation in Christ

3.6.1   Salvation comes from God's grace alone
received through faith in Christ.
From all eternity, and through no merit on our part,
God calls us to life in Christ.
Here is the good news of the Gospel!
Jesus Christ is the elect one,
chosen for our salvation.
In him we are made acceptable to God.
Before the world was made
we were chosen in Christ
to be part of the family of God.

3.6.2   We are called for a purpose:
we have been predestined
to be like Christ
and to serve God.
As with Israel in the Old Testament,
so with the new humanity in the New Testament,
God chooses us.
There is assurance in knowing that the living God
has eternal purposes to achieve through us.
God will bring to completion
the work of grace begun in us.

CHAPTER FOUR

God the Holy Spirit

4.1 The Holy Spirit is God with Us

4.1.1 The Holy Spirit is the Spirit of the triune God
and is One with the Father and the Son.
The Holy Spirit is the Lord and Giver of Life,
the Renewer and Helper of God's people.
By the Spirit, God is present in the world,
the source of all goodness and justice.
By the Spirit, God convinces the world of sin
and testifies to the truth of Christ.
By the Spirit, Christ is with his church.

4.2 The Holy Spirit Enables People to Believe

4.2.1 The Spirit enables people to receive
the good news of Christ,
to repent of their sins,
and to be adopted as children of God.
As we hear and respond to the Gospel
we freely turn to Christ.
When we have turned and repented,
we recognize that the Spirit enabled us to believe.

4.2.2 The Holy Spirit accompanies us on our journey of faith.
We may not always be sure of this presence.
Yet God's Spirit is with us,
sometimes gently, sometimes powerfully,
guiding us in the midst of life,
our comfort and our help.
Christian life is a pilgrimage:
it begins, continues, and ends in God.

4.3 The Holy Spirit Forms and Equips the Church

4.3.1 By the Spirit, Christ calls the church into being
and unites us to himself and to each other.
The Holy Spirit is in all who know Christ.

4.3.2 The Holy Spirit is the Spirit of truth.
We pray as a church to be guided into truth
knowing that such truth may disturb and judge us.

4.3.3   The presence of the Holy Spirit is seen
         in love,
         joy, peace, patience, kindness,
         goodness, loyalty, gentleness, and self-control.

4.3.4   The Spirit blesses us with various gifts.
         We seek to discover those gifts
         and to use them for our Lord.
         Faithful loving service is a sign
         that the Spirit is present.
         The presence of the Spirit is evident
         where people are made whole, encouraged,
         and enabled to grow in Christ.

4.3.5   Come, Holy Spirit!

CHAPTER FIVE   *The Bible*

5.1   The Bible has been given to us
         by the inspiration of God
         to be the rule of faith and life.
         It is the standard of all doctrine
         by which we must test any word that comes to us
         from church, world, or inner experience.
         We subject to its judgement
         all we believe and do.
         Through the Scriptures
         the church is bound only to Jesus Christ its King and Head.
         He is the living Word of God
         to whom the written word bears witness.

5.2   The Holy Spirit gives us inner testimony
         to the unique authority of the Bible
         and is the source of its power.
         The Bible, written by human hands,
         is nonetheless the word of God
         as no other word ever written.
         To it no other writings are to be added.
         The Scriptures are necessary, sufficient, and reliable,
         revealing Jesus Christ, the living Word.

5.3   Both Old and New Testaments were written
         within communities of faith

and accepted as Scripture by them.
Those who seek to understand the Bible
need to stand within the church
and listen to its teaching.

5.4 The Bible is to be understood in the light
of the revelation of God's work in Christ.
The writing of the Bible was conditioned
by the language, thought,
and setting of its time.
The Bible must be read in its historical context.
We interpret Scripture
as we compare passages,
seeing the two Testaments in light of each other,
and listening to commentators past and present.
Relying on the Holy Spirit,
we seek the application of God's word for our time.

CHAPTER SIX

6.1 Faith

6.1.1 Faith is a gift of God
constantly renewed in Word and Sacrament
and in the shared life of God's people.
It is trust in God,
involves personal repentance of sin,
acceptance of Jesus Christ as Saviour,
and commitment to him as Lord.
It includes assent
to the truth of the Gospel.
By faith we receive the very life of God
into our lives
and joyfully discover
that God knows, loves, and pardons us.

6.1.2 God brings us to faith in many ways.
We may have trusted in God from childhood;
or our faith may have come later in life.
Faith may come suddenly
or only after a struggle to believe.
Whatever the spiritual journey we have travelled,
God honours our faith, great or small.

6.1.3   Faith is a response
to God's presence in the midst of life.
It says "yes" to the God who is here.

6.2   **Doubt**

6.2.1   We are not always certain that God is with us.
At times God calls us
to live in this world
without experiencing the divine presence,
often discerning God's nearness
only as we look back.
At other times God seems absent
in order that our faith may be tested.
Through such struggle we mature in faith.
God may also chasten and strengthen us
through the hard circumstances of life.

6.2.2   Questioning may be a sign of growth.
It may also be disobedience:
we must be honest with ourselves.
Since we are to love God with our minds,
as well as our hearts,
the working through of doubt
is part of our growth in faith.
The church includes many who struggle with doubt.
Jesus accepted the man who prayed:
"Lord, I believe. Help my unbelief."

6.2.3   Though the strength of our faith may vary
and in many ways be assailed and weakened,
yet we may find assurance in Christ
through confidence in his word,
the sacraments of his church,
and the work of his Spirit.

CHAPTER SEVEN   *God's Church*

7.1   **The Church**

7.1.1   The church is Christ
together with his people

called both to worship and to serve him
in all of life.

7.1.2 The church is **one.**
It is one family under God whose purpose it is
to unite all people in Jesus Christ.

7.1.3 The church is **holy.**
It is set apart by God through the Holy Spirit
to be a chosen people in the world.

7.1.4 The church is **catholic.**
It is universal, including all people of all time
who affirm the Christian Faith.

7.1.5 The church is **apostolic.**
It is founded on Christ and the apostles
and is in continuity with their teachings.

7.1.6 The church is in constant need of reform
because of the failure and sin
which mark its life in every age.
The church is present
when the Word is truly preached,
the sacraments rightly administered,
and as it orders its life
according to the word of God.

7.2 **Ministry**

7.2.1 The Lord continues his ministry
in and through the church.
All Christians are called
to participate in the ministry of Christ.
As his body on earth
we all have gifts to use
in the church and in the world
to the glory of Christ, our King and Head.

7.2.2 Through the church God orders this ministry
by calling some to special tasks
in the equipping of the saints
for the work of ministry,
for building up the body of Christ.

7.2.3   Ministers of Word and Sacrament
are set apart to preach the Gospel,
celebrate Baptism and Holy Communion
and exercise pastoral care in Christ's name.
Their ministry is an order
which continues the work of the apostles.
Christ preserves this order today
by calling to it both men and women.
The church recognizes this calling
in the act of ordination.

7.2.4   Through the office of ruling elder
men and women are ordained
to share with the minister
in the leadership, pastoral care,
and oversight of the congregation.

7.2.5   Specialized ministries are recognized
through the designation of
deaconesses and church educators,
professors and administrators,
missionaries and catechists,
chaplains and counsellors.

7.2.6   Through such ministries
the Word is proclaimed,
God's people are nourished and nurtured,
supported and guided.
In the oneness of Christ
we seek to serve God.

7.3   Worship

7.3.1   The church lives to praise God.
We have no higher calling
than to offer the worship that belongs to God
day by day, Sunday by Sunday.

7.3.2   Through the preaching of the Word
and the celebration of the Sacraments,
in praise, prayer, teaching and fellowship,
God sustains the life of the church.
We worship God as Lord
offering ourselves in the service of Christ,
rejoicing that we have been brought from darkness to light.

7.3.3   Worship draws us into the work of Christ.
Even now he intercedes for the world
to which he came and for which he died.
In union with him, the church prays
for the healing and the salvation of the world.

7.3.4   Blessing and honour and glory and power
be to our God for ever and ever!

7.4   Preaching

7.4.1   To the church and to the world
Christ sends ambassadors to preach the good news.
The reconciling work of Jesus
was the supreme turning point in the life of the world.
The proclamation of his cross and resurrection
calls for personal response
and offers present hope.
The Holy Spirit enables God's Word to be heard
in the word of preaching.
Faith comes by hearing, and
by preaching it is continually renewed.

7.4.2   Preachers must be servants of the Word;
those who listen should pray
for those who speak.
They must be hungry to hear what the Lord has to say.
The spoken word is food for all believers.

7.5   Sacraments

7.5.1   In obedience to our Lord's command and example
we observe two sacraments,
Baptism and Holy Communion.
These are visible expressions of the Gospel
given as means of entering and sustaining the Christian Life.

7.5.2   In Baptism and the Lord's Supper,
there is a sacramental union
between the sign and the thing signified.
Water signifies forgiveness and new life in Christ;
bread and wine, the body and blood of our Lord.

7.5.3   The grace effective in the sacraments
comes not from any power in them

but from the work of the Holy Spirit.
Rightly received, in faith and repentance,
the sacraments convey that which they symbolize.

7.6   **Baptism**

7.6.1   Baptism is a sign and seal of our union with Christ
and with his church.
Through it we share
in the death and resurrection of Christ
and are commissioned to his service.

7.6.2   In Baptism, water is administered
in the name of the Father,
and of the Son,
and of the Holy Spirit.
The water signifies the washing away of sin,
the start of new life in Christ,
and the gift of the Holy Spirit.

7.6.3   By the power of the Holy Spirit
God acts through Baptism.
It is the sacrament not of what we do
but of what God has done for us in Christ.
God's grace and our response to it
are not tied to the moment of Baptism,
but continue and deepen throughout life.
It is a sacrament meant
for those who profess their faith
and for their children.
Together we are the family of God.

7.6.4   Baptism is also an act of discipleship
that requires commitment
and looks towards growth in Christ.
Those baptized in infancy
are called in later years
to make personal profession of Christ.
What is born may die.
What is grafted may wither.
Congregations and those baptized
must strive to nurture life in Christ.

7.6.5   Baptism assures us that we belong to God.
In life and in death

our greatest comfort is that we belong
to our faithful Saviour Jesus Christ.

7.7   **Holy Communion**

7.7.1   In breaking bread and drinking wine
Jesus told us to remember him.
In this action
called Holy Communion, Lord's Supper, or Eucharist,
Christ offers himself to us
and we present ourselves to him
in worship and adoration.

7.7.2   In Holy Communion
Christ places his table in this world
to feed and bless his people.
The Holy Spirit so unites us in Christ
that in receiving the bread and wine in faith
we share in his body and blood.

7.7.3   The Lord's Supper is a joyful mystery
whereby Jesus takes the bread and wine
to represent his atoning sacrifice,
deepening our union with himself
and with each other,
giving us of his life and strength.
Here Christ is present in his world
proclaiming salvation until he comes—
a symbol of hope for a troubled age.

7.7.4   The Eucharist is thanksgiving to God.
We pray for the world
and with gratitude offer our lives to God.
We celebrate his victory over death
and anticipate the joyous feast we shall have
in his coming kingdom.
We pledge allegiance to Christ as Lord,
are fed as one church,
receive these signs of his love,
and are marked as his.

7.7.5   Those who belong to Christ come gladly to his table
to make a memorial of his life and death,
to celebrate his presence,
and together as his church offer him thanks.

CHAPTER EIGHT *Our Life in Christ*

8.1   **Discipleship**

8.1.1   Disciples of Christ are called to obedience.
         Jesus said: "If you love me, keep my commandments."
         Obedience involves us totally.
         Yet as we give ourselves to him we discover
         that his service alone brings true freedom.

8.1.2   Life in Christ is formed in a believing community,
         and expressed in daily living.
         We are to bring Christ's healing presence
         to the world for which he died,
         his peace to its pain and anguish.

8.1.3   Life in Christ brings joy, liberty, glory.
         But it also brings conflict
         with unbelief, fear, and temptation.
         Throughout our lives
         we struggle with disheartening difficulties.
         Yet the Holy Spirit helps us
         and gives us power to grow in Christ.
         While we are far from perfect
         yet our lives can be pleasing to God
         and helpful to others.

8.1.4   Life in Christ involves prayer,
         the seeking of God's will and blessing
         on all of life.
         Prayer is openness to the presence of God.
         In words, or the absence of words,
         prayer is the focusing of our lives towards God.
         As we commune with God through Jesus Christ,
         the Holy Spirit enables us to express our deepest longings,
         and we experience the sustaining power of God's presence.

8.1.5   We live in Christ as we study the Scriptures
         learning to think and act in a Christian way.
         The Scriptures are given that Christians may be complete,
         equipped for every good work.

8.1.6   We live in Christ as in freedom we observe Sunday

22

as the weekly festival of the resurrection,
for the worship of our Lord, rest from our work,
and the enjoyment of God's world.

8.2   **The Christian Family**

8.2.1   All Christians are members both of a human family
          and of the church, the household of God.
          We honour our parents who gave us life,
          and also the church which has nurtured us in the faith.

8.2.2   God's purpose for us can be realized
          in both single and married life.
          Marriage is not God's will for everyone.
          Fullness of life is offered to all,
          both single and married.

8.2.3   Christian marriage is a union in Christ
          whereby a man and a woman become one in the sight of God.
          It is the commitment of two people
          to love and to support one another faithfully for life.
          God's law forbids adultery.
          Loyalty is necessary for the growth of love.
          Disloyalty destroys the union of marriage.
          Sexual union in marriage is intended to provide
          mutual joy and comfort as well as
          the means of creating new life.

8.2.4   Parents in caring for their children
          are mediators of God's love and discipline.
          They are called to raise their children
          within the covenant community,
          to be faithful to vows taken at Baptism
          to nurture them in the Faith
          by teaching and example.

8.2.5   When we fail each other as parents or partners,
          we are called to forgive each other as God forgives us,
          and to accept the possibilities for renewal
          that God offers us in grace.
          When a marriage is shattered beyond repair,
          it is sometimes better that it be dissolved
          than that the family continue to live in bitterness.

8.2.6   The church is the family of God.
Here all should be valued for themselves.
We are one body in Christ:
together rejoicing when things go well,
supporting one another in sorrow,
celebrating the goodness of God
and the wonder of our redemption.

8.3   Love

8.3.1   We bow before the mystery of God's love.
From it came our creation.
By it we are daily nurtured.
Through it we find salvation.
A consuming fire of purity, God's love
is yet warm and gentle compassion.
We respond to the God who is love
by loving in return.

8.3.2   Love means seeking the best for others
and is the mark of a Christian.
Love for God leads to love for others.
We cannot claim to love God, whom we do not see,
if we hate those about us, whom we do see.
Love of God and of neighbour fulfils the law of God.

8.3.3   Love is compassion for creation.
Love is the service of others and is not self-centred.
Love speaks the truth tempered with kindness.
Love grows in knowledge and discernment.
It is the road to Christian maturity, and is
the way of seeing others as God sees them.
Love follows the example of Jesus Christ.

8.3.4   We should also love ourselves.
Self-love is not selfishness.
We love and accept ourselves because
God has already loved and accepted us in Christ,
providing the foundation of our sense of worth.

8.3.5   Love is the greatest gift in the world
because it will last beyond this world
and is supremely pleasing to our Lord.
Love foreshadows life in heaven.

8.4   **Justice**

8.4.1   God is always calling the church
           to seek that justice in the world
           which reflects the divine righteousness
           revealed in the Bible.

8.4.2   God's justice is seen
           when we deal fairly with each other
           and strive to change customs and practices
           that oppress and enslave others.

8.4.3   Justice involves protecting the rights of others.
           It protests against everything that destroys human dignity.

8.4.4   Justice requires concern for the poor of the world.
           It seeks the best way to create
           well-being in every society.
           It is concerned about employment, education, and health,
           as well as rights and responsibilities.

8.4.5   Justice seeks fairness in society.
           It involves the protection of human beings,
           concern for the victims of crime,
           as well as offenders.
           It requires fair laws justly administered,
           courts and penal institutions that are just and humane.

8.4.6   Justice opposes prejudice in every form.
           It rejects discrimination
           on such grounds as race, sex, age, status, or handicap.
           Justice stands with our neighbours
           in their struggle for dignity and respect
           and demands the exercise of power for the common good.

8.5   **World Peace**

8.5.1   Christ, the Prince of Peace,
           calls his followers to seek peace in the world.

8.5.2   We know that nations have fought in self-defence
           and that war, at times, may be unavoidable.
           But the tragic evil that comes with war,
           the slaughter of men, women, and children
           must rouse us to work for peace.

8.5.3   We protest against the world arms race
that diminishes our ability to fight
hunger, ignorance, poverty and disease.
We fear nuclear war
and the devastation it would bring.
We affirm that God is at work when people are
ashamed of the inhumanity of war
and work for peace with justice.
We pray for peace
to him who is the Prince of Peace.

CHAPTER NINE

The Church Reaches Out

9.1   **Our Mission**

9.1.1   As God sent Christ to us,
so Christ sends us into the world.
We are here to proclaim Christ in word and deed.

9.1.2   Mission is evangelism,
the offer of salvation to all people
in the power of the Holy Spirit,
to be received through faith in Christ.
It asks people to repent of their sins,
to trust Christ,
to be baptized,
and to enter a life honouring Jesus as Lord.

9.1.3   Mission is service,
a call to help people in need and
to permeate all of life with the compassion of God.

9.2   **Our Mission and Other Faiths**

9.2.1   Some whom we encounter belong to other religions
and already have a faith.
Their lives often give evidence of devotion
and reverence for life.
We recognize that truth and goodness in them
are the work of God's Spirit, the author of all truth.
We should not address others in a spirit of arrogance

implying that we are better than they.
But rather, in the spirit of humility,
as beggars telling others where food is to be found,
we point to life in Christ.

9.2.2   We witness to God in Christ
as the Way, the Truth, the Life,
and invite others to accept from him
the forgiveness of God.
We are compelled to share this good news.

9.3   Our Mission and Unbelief

9.3.1   For some today "God" is an empty word
indicating no reality
they have ever consciously known.
They do not believe there is a God.

9.3.2   Many find it hard to believe in a loving God
in a world where so many suffer.
Unbelief threatens many with despair,
the feeling that nothing really matters
and that beyond this world is emptiness.

9.3.3   The Bible witnesses to God in Christ
entering deeply into human suffering.
As we behold our Saviour on the cross,
we are convinced of God's love for us.
Faced with the pain and agony of the world,
only a suffering God can help.
God is with us in our anguish.

9.3.4   Faithful men and women of the Bible
also knew pain and uncertainty.
Yet they experienced God and felt compelled
to speak of God moving powerfully in life.
Christian faith is a response
to the searching presence of God.
Christian belief brings new meaning
into one's life,
for life's true purpose
is to glorify and to enjoy God.

CHAPTER TEN

Our Hope in God

10.1   God has prepared for us
        things beyond our imagining.
        Our hope is for a renewed world
        and for fullness of life in the age to come.
        As Jesus taught us, we pray:
        "Thy kingdom come."

10.2   Life in the age to come
        is pictured in the Bible in different ways:
        an eternal kingdom,
        a new heaven and earth,
        a marriage feast,
        an unending day,
        the father's house,
        and the joy of God's presence.
        God will triumph over all opposition
        and everything that disrupts creation.

10.3   We shall all stand under the final judgement of God,
        as we receive the divine verdict on our lives.
        Worthy of hell, eternal separation from God,
        our hope is for heaven, eternal life with God
        through the grace bestowed on us in Christ.
        To say "no" to Christ is to refuse life
        and to embrace death.
        The destiny of all people
        is in the hands of God
        whose mercy and justice we trust.

10.4   Eternal life is resurrection life.
        As God raised Christ,
        so shall we be raised
        into a condition fit for life with God.
        Eternal life begins in this life:
        whoever believes in the Son of God
        already has eternal life.
        In Baptism by faith we die and rise with Christ
        and so are one with the risen Lord.
        In death we commit our future confidently to God.

10.5   Life had its beginning in God.
        In God it will come to completion
        and its meaning be fully revealed.
        All creation will find fulfilment in God.
        Christ will come again.
        Only God knows when and how
        our Lord will return.
        Now we see in part.
        Then we shall see face to face.

10.6   Come, Lord Jesus!

10.7   May the God of hope
        fill us with joy and peace in believing
        so that by the power of the Holy Spirit
        we abound in hope!

>off

SCRIPTURAL REFERENCES

The following Scriptural passages are an Appendix to LIVING FAITH and invite the reader to turn to the Old and New Testaments as the source of Christian truth. This is not an exhaustive list of the relevant passages. It is a means by which the inquirer may find some of the texts with which the authors of this statement have wrestled in its preparation. LIVING FAITH is offered as a faithful and obedient interpretation of the Scriptures.

References are given so that they may be studied in relation to chapters, sections, or subsections. The text used in preparing the Scriptural references is that of the Revised Standard Version.

Chapter One: **GOD.**
PSALM 50:1-6, ISAIAH 40:18-31, MICAH 7:18-20, MATTHEW 6:1-34, JOHN 3:16, COLOSSIANS 1:3-8, 2 CORINTHIANS 13:14.

1.1 Jer.10:10, Jn.17:3, 2 Tim.1:8-10, Ps.100:1-2, Rom.14:17, Ps.148:1-5, Rev.4:11, Ps.19:1-6, Ps.102:24-7, Rev.15:1-4.
1.2 Gen.3:8-9, Jn.1:14, Ex.19:1-20:21, Deut.29:29, Ex.2:23-5, Ps.111:9-10, Mt.1:1, 2 Tim.2:8, Mk.1:1, Lk.3:22, Jer.31:31-34, 1 Cor.11:23-5, Rom.5:1, Rom.10:4-9, Lk.3:16, 2 Cor.3:17-18, Acts 1:4-5, 1 Cor.2:12-16, Acts 16:6-10, Gal.6:14-16.
1.3 1 Tim.3:14-16, 2 Tim.1:13-14, Eph.3:1-6, 2 Pet.1:16-18, 1 Cor.2:12-13, Ps.106:1-48, Acts 2:14-36, Ps.99:6-9, Jn.17:25-6, Jn.20:31.
1.4 Gal.1:1-4, 1 Cor.15:1-4, Acts 2:42, 1 Jn.4:1-6, Eph.2:20, 2 Th.2:15, Rom.16:17-18, 2 Pet.3:14-18, Heb.13:7-9.
1.5 Eph.4:1-6, Rev.7:9-12, Mt.28:19, 2 Cor.13:14, Mk.1:9-11, 1 Jn.4:13-14, Rom.1:1-4, Eph. 2:18, Jn.16:15, 1 Cor.2:7-11, Mt.6:9, 1 Pet.1:17, Jn.14:6, Heb.4:14-16, 1 Cor.12:3, Jude 20-1.
1.6 Ps.95:1-11, Acts 17:24-8, Ps.107:1-43, Col.3:16-17, Ps.85:1-13, 1 Cor.1:27-31, Jn.5:22-3, Rom.16:25-7, Rom.8:26-7, Eph.3:14-21, 1 Tim.1:17, Heb.13:20-21, Jude 24-5, Rev.5:11-14.

Chapter Two: **GOD, CREATOR AND RULER**
GENESIS 1:1-31, PSALM 145:1-21, COLOSSIANS 1:15-20.

2.1 **God Creates and Rules**
Psalm 33:4-19, Amos 1:1-3:8, Romans 11:33-6.
2.1.1 Ps.89:5-14, Ps.136:3-9, Gen.8:21-2, Is.10:5-27, Rom.11:22, Mt.10:29-31, Is.46:8-10.
2.1.2 Ps.103:19-22, Ps.102:12-28, Gen.50:20, Ps.2:1-11, Deut.30:19, Acts 2:22-3, Ps.113:5-9, Rom.8:28, Rev.11:15.
2.1.3 Rom.5:20, Rom.2:4-11, Gen.6:11-2, Rom.3:21-6, Mt.12:15-21, 2 Cor.8:9, 2 Cor.12:8-10.
2.1.4 Rom.9:14-28, Is.55:8-9, Job 14:1-2, 1 Cor.15:25-6, Col.3:1-3.
2.2 **Our Creation**
Genesis 1:26-8, Genesis 2:18-24, Psalm 8:1-9.
2.2.1 Ps.139:13-18, Gen.1:26, Acts 17:28, Mt.18:1-3, 1 Cor.3:18-23, Jas.3:13-18, Ps.145:10, Ps.147:7-11.
2.2.2 Gen.1:27, Ps.148:12-13, 1 Cor.11:11-12, Lk.8:1-3, Phil.4:1-3.
2.3 **Our Calling**
Job 28:28, Matthew 22:35-40, Mark 8:34-38.
2.3.1 Phil.2:12, Mk.12:28-31.
2.3.2 Deut.11:8-15, Eccl.11:6, Ps.41:1, 1 Cor.7:17, 2 Th.3:10-13, Eph.4:28.

2.3.3	Mk.10:35–45, Lk.9:57–62, Jas.3:16, Jn.8:36.
2.4	**Our Care for the World**
	Genesis 1:27–31, Genesis 2:15, Deuteronomy 8:7–20.
2.4.1	Acts 17:24–5, Ps.65:9–13, Ps.24:1, Jn.6:12, Ps.8:4–6.
2.4.2	Is.1:17, Mt.5:6, 2 Cor.8:12–15.
2.5	**Sin Separates Us From God**
	Genesis 3:22–4, Psalm 51:1–14, Matthew 15:10–20, Romans 1:18–3:20.
2.5.1	1 Jn.1:8–9, Lk.12:16–19, Ps.143:1–2, Neh.1:5–7, Ex.32:30–1, 1 Jn.3:4, Judg.21:25.
2.5.2	Ex.20:1–17, Mic.6:8, Rom.7:21–4, Rev.2:4, Mt.12:35–7, Jn.15:22, Jn.8:29.
2.5.3	Is.53:6, Is.6:1–5, Jn.13:30, Rom.6:21, Jer.17:9, Gal.5:19–21, Is.57:20–1.
2.5.4	Ps.58:3, Jn.8:34, Jas.1:14–15, Ezek.16:48–9, Lk.18:2–4, Prov.6:6–19, Mk.7:21–3.
2.5.5	Rom.3:19–20,23, Gal.3:22.
2.5.6	Jer.9:1–3, Ps.46:6, Lk.10:13–15, 1 Cor.1:19–20, Jer.3:25, Ps.130:1–4.
2.5.7	Tit.3:3, Rom.2:1–2, Acts 13:26, 1 Cor.2:2, Rom.4:25, Acts 13:38, 1 Cor.1:30–1, Tit.2:11–14, Rom.5:1.
2.5.8	1 Cor.15:56–7.

Chapter Three:	**GOD IN CHRIST**	
	ISAIAH 11:1–5, MATTHEW 16:16, 2 CORINTHIANS 5:10–21, HEBREWS 1:1–2:18, REVELATION 11:15–19.	

3.1	**Jesus Christ and Israel**
	Matthew 5:17–18, Mark 7:5–9, Luke 4:16–23, John 12:12–16.
3.1.1	Gen.6:11–12, Hab.2:14, Gen.12:1–3, Deut.29:10–15, Is.49:5–6.
3.1.2	Ex.12:25–7, Deut.4:5–8, Ps.126:3, Jer.3:14–18,4:5–8, Rom.16:25–6, Dan.7:13–14, Mic.5:2.
3.1.3	Mt.1:1, Mk.1:14–15, Rom.1:1–2, Acts 13:22–3, Lk.2:25–32, Is.60:1–3, Jn.8:12.
3.2	**Jesus Christ: Truly God**
	John 1:1–14, John 20:28, 1 Corinthians 8:6, Philippians 2:5–11, Colossians 2:8–9.
3.2.1	Jn.1:14, Heb.1:1–13, Lk.1:30–8, 2 Cor.1:18–20, Lk.1:35, Mt.1:22–5, Jn.17:5, 2 Cor.8:9, Heb.2:18, Rom.15:7–12, 2 Cor.5:19.
3.2.2	Jn.1:49, Col.1:19, Jn.1:18, Heb.1:5–13, Jn.14:8–9, Mt.11:25–7.
3.2.3	2 Cor.4:4, Rev.19:11–13, Col.1:15–16, Jn.1:4–5.
3.2.4	Acts 10:36, Jn.10:30, Rom.8:9–10.
3.3	**Jesus Christ: Truly Human**
	Luke 2:1–7, Mark 14:1–15:47, Hebrews 5:7–10.
3.3.1	Heb.2:17, Mt.4:1–11, Heb.4:15, Mk.14:33–4, Lk.22:28–30, Lk.19:41–2, Jn.19:31–42, Mk.14:36, Lk.4:14–18, Lk.13:31–3, Jn.14:30–1, Jn.15:13–15, Lk.2:41–52.
3.4	**Jesus is Saviour**
	Luke 2:11, Philippians 3:20–1, 1 John 4:14.
3.4.1	1 Tim.2:5, 1 Jn.1:1–3, Jn.16:24.
3.4.2	1 Cor.15:3, 2 Cor.5:20–1, 1 Pet.4:1, Jn.1:29.
3.4.3	Eph.3:1–5, Acts 8:32–5, Jn.10:11, Heb.7:26–7, 1 Pet.3:18, Mk.10:45, Rom.5:19, Col.2:15, 1 Jn.4:8, Is.53:1–12, Eph.3:19, Rom.5:1–11.
3.5	**Jesus is Lord**
	Acts 2:22–36, 1 Corinthians 15:1–11, Revelation 1:12–19.
3.5.1	Mk.15:37–42, Acts 13:30, 1 Pet.3:22, Rom.14:9.
3.5.2	1 Cor.15:12–25, 1Pet.5:8–9, 2 Tim.1:10.
3.5.3	Eph.4:27, 2 Cor.2:10–11, 1 Jn.3:8, 2 Th.1:4–10.
3.5.4	Rev.1:4–5,7:9–12, Heb.9:24, Rom.8:34, Heb.13:15, 1 Tim.2:1–4.
3.5.5	1 Cor.15:57, 2 Cor.2:14.
3.6	**Salvation in Christ**
	Matthew 12:15–21, Ephesians 1:1–14, Titus 2:11–14.
3.6.1	Tit.3:3–8, Eph.2:8, 2 Tim.1:8–9, Jn.10:10, Rom.11:5–6, Lk.3:22, 1 Pet.2:3–7,

3.6.2	Col.2:9–10, Eph.1:4–5, Heb.2:11–13. Jn.15:16, Rom.8:29, Jn.12:25–6, Is.43:1–7, 2 Th.2:13–14, Col.3:12–14, Rom.3:21–4, Ps.138:8, Phil.1:6, Jas.1:18.

Chapter Four: **GOD THE HOLY SPIRIT**
PSALM 104:30, JOEL 2:28–9, ZECHARIAH 4:6, MARK 3:20–30,
JOHN 14:15–16:16.

4.1   **The Holy Spirit is God with us**
Psalm 139:7–12, Luke 3:15–16, 1 John 3:24.
4.1.1   1 Cor.2:9–16, Eph.4:4–6, Acts 4:31, Gen.1:2, Mic.3:8, Jn.16:7–11,
Eph.1:13–14,4:1–3
4.2   **The Holy Spirit Enables People to Believe**
Acts 11:19–21, Romans 8:14–16, 1 Corinthians 2:1–5.
4.2.1   1 Th.1:5, Acts 11:15–18,16:14, Gal.4:4–7, Jn.8:30, Lk.15:17–20, Rom.9:16, 1
Cor.12:3.
4.2.2   Is.59:21, Job 23:1–3, Eph.4:30, Jn.3:7–8, Acts 10:19–20, 1 Jn.2:20–27, Heb.13:14,
Rev.22:12–14.
4.3   **The Holy Spirit Forms and Equips the Church**
Acts 2:1–21, Ephesians 2:19–21, 1 Peter 1:1–2.
4.3.1   Rom.15:18–19, Phil.2:1–3, Rom.8:1–2,9.
4.3.2   Jn.14:15–17, Ps.5:7–8, Rev.3:14–22.
4.3.3   Gal.5:22–3.
4.3.4   1 Cor.12:4–7, Rom.12:6, 1 Pet.4:10–11, Rom.12:9–13, Acts 8:5–8,19:1–20.
4.3.5   Lk.11:13.

Chapter Five: **THE BIBLE**
PSALM 119:97–112,162–176, ROMANS 15:4, 2 TIMOTHY
3:14–17, 2 PETER 1:20–1.

5.1   Mt.22:43–4, Heb.3:7–11, Mt.4:4,7,10, Jer.23:26–32, Deut.13:1–4, 1 Jn.4:1–6,
Gal.4:21–31, Acts 17:10–11, Jn.5:39, Rom.16:25–7, Jn.1:1, 1 Jn.2:21.
5.2   Acts 5:30–2, 1 Pet.1:10–12, Heb.4:12, Jer.36:4, Ps.19:7–11, Rev.22:18–19, 2
Tim.3:16, 2 Cor.4:5.
5.3   Deut.31:9, Lk.1:1–4, Rom.16:21–3, Col.4:7–18, 2 Pet.3:15–16, Ps.119:18, 1
Cor.11:16, 2 Pet.1:20–1, 1 Cor.14:29,37.
5.4   Jn.20:31, 2 Tim.2:8-10,14, Ruth 4:7–12, Ps.104:26, Gen.17:9–14, Lk.3:1–2, 2
Tim.2:15, Acts 7:1–50, Heb.11:1–40, Ps.106:1–48, 1 Cor.10:1–13, Eph.1:15–19,
Jas.1:22.

Chapter Six: **FAITH**
GENESIS 15:1–6, MATTHEW 8:5–13, JOHN 14:1–14, HEBREWS
3:12–4:11.

6.1   **Faith**
Matthew 15:21–8, Romans 4:1–25, Hebrews 11:1–12:2.
6.1.1   Eph.2:8, Acts 2:37–42, Mk.11:22, Lk.13:1–5, Jn.4:39–42, Col.2:6–7, 1 Th.2:13,
Jn.3:14–15, Acts 16:27–34.
6.1.2   Mt.18:1–6, Lk.19:1–10, Acts 9:3–6, Jn.20:24–8, Acts 2:21.
6.1.3   Jn.11:25–7, Gen.28:16–21.
6.2   **Doubt**
Job 3:1–26, Psalm 77:1–10, Matthew 14:22–33, 2 Corinthians 4:8–9.
6.2.1   2 Cor.7:5, Lam.1:1–3:18, Ps.119:67,71,75, 2 Chr.32:31, 1 Pet.1:6–7, Heb.12:4–11.

6.2.2	Mk.9:9–10, Ps.78:19, 2 Cor.13:5, Mt.22:37, Ps.111:1, Lk.7:18–23, Gal.1:1–6, Mk.9:24.
6.2.3	Gal.5:7, Num.21:4–5, Heb.6:11–12, Mk.13:31, Col.2:10–14, 1 Jn.5:4–7.

Chapter Seven: **GOD'S CHURCH**
PSALM 122:1–9, HOSEA 2:19–23, MATTHEW 16:13–19, 1 PETER 2:4–10.

7.1	**The Church**
	John 10:14–16, Acts 9:31, Ephesians 2:1–10,19–22, 1 Timothy 3:14–16.
7.1.1	Mt.18:20, Col.3:24,17, Mt.28:17.
7.1.2	Eph.4:4–6, Gal.3:25–9.
7.1.3	1 Cor.3:16–17, 1 Pet.1:1–2.
7.1.4	Ps.107:1–3, Col.3:9–11, Jude 3.
7.1.5	Acts 2:42, Eph.2:20, Jn.17:6–23.
7.1.6	Rev.2:5, Jas.4:1–4, 2 Cor.3:2–3, Mk.16:20, 1 Cor.10:16–17, Lk.11:27–8.
7.2	**Ministry**
	Mark 10:35–45, Ephesians 4:8–16, 1 Timothy 3:1–13.
7.2.1	Jn.20:21, Rom.12:4–9, 1 Cor.12:12–27, Phil.2:14–16, 1 Pet.4:10–11, Heb.13:20–1.
7.2.2	Acts 13:1–3, Col.4:17, Eph.4:12, Rom.1:11–12.
7.2.3	Heb.13:7, Acts 20:28, 2 Tim.2:1–2, 1 Th.5:12–13, Acts 2:18–19, 1 Tim.4:14.
7.2.4	Acts 14:23, 1 Cor.12:28, Rom.12:6–8.
7.2.5	1 Cor.12:4–7.
7.2.6	2 Tim.4:1–5, Jn.21:15–17, Jn.15:12, 1 Pet.2:16.
7.3	**Worship**
	Psalm 84:1–12, Ephesians 5:15–20, Revelation 15:2–4.
7.3.1	Lk.24:52, Ps.48:9–10, Jn.4:23–4, Ps.145:2, Rev.1:10.
7.3.2	Mk.2:2, Acts 10:47–8,2:46–7, Is.41:17–18, Ps.96:7–9, Rom.12:1–2, 1 Pet.2:9.
7.3.3	2 Cor.6:1–2, Heb.7:24–5, 1 Jn.2:2, 1 Tim.2:1–4, Jn.12:28–32.
7.3.4	Rev.7:12.
7.4	**Preaching**
	Luke 24:44–9, Romans 10:4–17, 1 Corinthians 9:16, 2 Timothy 4:1–5.
7.4.1	Jn.20:19–23, 2 Cor.5:20, Col.1:19–20, Jn.12:31–2, 1 Cor.1:23–4, Acts 20:21, 1 Tim.1:1, 1 Cor.2:4, 1 Pet.1:25, Rom.10:17, Col.1:24–9.
7.4.2	2 Tim.2:14–16, Ps.85:8–9, Eph.6:18–19, Mt.5:6,4:4.
7.5	**Sacraments**
	Acts 2:37–42, 1 Corinthians 10:14–17.
7.5.1	Mk.16:15–16,14:22–3, Acts 18:8–11, Jn.6:52–9.
7.5.2	Acts 22:16, Lk.22:19–20.
7.5.3	Ps.51:15–17, Jn.6:63, 1 Pet.3:21.
7.6	**Baptism**
	Matthew 28:16–20, Galatians 3:26–7, 1 Peter 3:18–22.
7.6.1	1 Cor.12:13, Rom.6:1–4.
7.6.2	Acts 8:36–8, Mt.28:19, Lk.3:2–3, Col.2:12–13, Acts 19:4–6.
7.6.3	Lk.3:16, Lk.12:50, Jas.4:6–10, Acts 4:31–3,10,44–8, 1 Cor.7:14, Acts 2:39.
7.6.4	Mt.28:19–20, 2 Pet.3:18, Rom.14:12,10:9–10, Heb.6:4–6, Jn.15:6, 2 Cor.7:1.
7.6.5	Rom.14:8, Col.3:1–4, Jn.14:27.
7.7	**Holy Communion**
	Matthew 26:26–9, John 6:52–9, 1 Corinthians 11:23–32.
7.7.1	1 Cor.11:23–5, Mk.14:22–3, 1 Cor.5:6–8, 1 Pet.5:6–7.
7.7.2	Lk.24:30–1, 1 Cor.10:16.
7.7.3	Acts 2:42, Heb.9:27–8, Rev.3:20, Jn.15:1–10, 1 Cor.11:26, Mt.24:14.
7.7.4	Jn.6:11, 1 Tim.2:1–4, Col.3:5–17, Rom.6:9–11, Mt.8:11, Lk.14:15–24,22:15–16, Jn.13:13, 1 Cor.11:28, Ps.78:23–5.
7.7.5	1 Cor.10:17,31.

Chapter Eight: **OUR LIFE IN CHRIST**
JOHN 15:1–17, EPHESIANS 4:17–5:17, 1 JOHN 1:1–10.

8.1   **Discipleship**
John 13:1–17, Ephesians 6:1–18, Hebrews 10:19–25.
8.1.1   Jn.14:15, Phil.3:7–8, Jn.8:31–2.
8.1.2   Gal.2:20,5:13, Mt.10:16, Jas.3:17–18.
8.1.3   Phil.4:4–5,1:27–30, Rom.7:21–4,8:13, 1 Jn.1:8,3:22, Acts 18:27, 2 Cor.1:11.
8.1.4   Lk.18:1, Mt.6:10, Ps.139:1–6,62:1–8,116:1–19, Heb.4:14–16, Rom.8:15–17, Phil.4:6–7.
8.1.5   Ps.19:7–14, Jn.17:17, 2 Tim.3:16–17, Eph.6:17.
8.1.6   Mk.2:27, Acts 20:7, Is.58:13–14, Col.2:16.
8.2   **The Christian Family**
Mark 10:1–16, Ephesians 5:21–6:4, 1 Peter 3:1–12.
8.2.1   Gen.4:1, 1 Cor.1:2, Deut.5:16, 1 Cor.4:14–16.
8.2.2   1 Cor.7:17, Jer.16:1, Pr.18:22, Lk.18:29–30, Is.56:4–5.
8.2.3   Eph.5:21–33, Mk.10:7–9, Mt.18:19, 1 Th.4:1–8, Ex.20:14, Ps.85:10–11, Mal.2:13–16, Song.1:1–8:14, Gen.1:28.
8.2.4   Ezra 8:21, Eph.6:4, Deut.6:6–7, Ps.78:1–8, Heb.6:1–3, Prov.3:1–8, 1 Cor.11:1.
8.2.5   Gen.25:28, Eph.4:32, Gal.6:1–2, 1 Tim.1:15, 1 Cor.7:12–15.
8.2.6   Heb.3:6, 2 Cor.6:14–18, Jas.2:1–9, Rom.12:5,15, 2 Cor.1:3–4, Ps.104:1–35, 2 Tim.1:7–10.
8.3   **Love**
Psalm 26:8, Isaiah 49:14–15, 1 Corinthians 13:1–13.
8.3.1   Jn.5:20–3, 1 Jn.4:8, 2 Cor.5:14, 1 Jn.4:9–10, Heb.12:29, Rev.21:4–5, 1 Jn.4:19.
8.3.2   Jn.15:13,13:35, 1 Jn.4:21,20, Rom.13:10.
8.3.3   Ps.145:8–9, 2 Cor.12:14–15, Eph.4:15, 2 Th.3:5, Eph.3:17–19, Lk.10:33, Mk.8:34–6.
8.3.4   1 Tim.4:16, Mk.10:28–30, 1 Cor.4:1–4, Eph.1:5–6, Mt.6:25–33.
8.3.5   1 Cor.13:13, Jn.15:17, 1 Jn.2:17, 1 Pet.4:8, Ps.73:24–6.
8.4   **Justice**
Psalm 15:1–5, Amos 5:1–24, Matthew 5:6.
8.4.1   Gen.18:22–5, Prov.14:34, Is.45:8,23,24, Jer.9:23–4.
8.4.2   Ps.9:7–8, Jer.22:15–16, Ex.9:1, Lk.4:18.
8.4.3   Deut.15:7–11, Hab.2:5–20.
8.4.4   Ps.41:1, Is.1:16–17, Prov.8:1–21, Mt.20:1–7, Pr.4:1–19, 3 Jn.1–2.
8.4.5   Lev.19:11, Zech.7:8–10, Job 24:1–4:13–17, Philemon 1–25, Neh.5:1–13, 2 Sam.23:1–4.
8.4.6   Prov.24:23–5, Lev.19:13–16, Mt.25:31–40,18:31, Ex.18:21–2, Ps.72:1–7.
8.5   **World Peace**
Proverbs 3:13–17, Micah 4:1–4, Luke 2:13–14.
8.5.1   Jn.12:14–15, Mt.5:9.
8.5.2   2 Chr.20:1–30, Mk.13:7, Ps.74:4–11, Am.1:13, Heb.12:14.
8.5.3   Mt.26:52, Is.55:2, Lk.9:1–2, 2 Pet.3:10, Lk.23:29–31, Ps.46:9,120:6–7, Jas.3:18, 3 Jn.15, Is.9:5–6.

Chapter Nine: **THE CHURCH REACHES OUT**
PSALM 67:1–7, MATTHEW 9:36–8, EPHESIANS 3:8.

9.1   **Our Mission**
John 10:16, Acts 1:6–8, 1 Thessalonians 1:1–10.
9.1.1   Gal.4:4, Mt.5:13–15, Jas.1:22.
9.1.2   Acts 8:4, Tit.2:11–14, 1 Cor.4:20, Acts 13:38–9, Mk.6:12, Jn.14:1, Acts 10:48, Col.1:9–10.
9.1.3   Gal.5:13, 1 Jn.3:17–18, Mt.5:7.

9.2 **Our Mission and Other Faiths**
Joshua 24:14–15, Acts 4:12, 2 Corinthians 3:12–18.
9.2.1 Is.37:37–8, Acts 8:27–8, Acts 10:1–2, Lk.10:33–4, Rom.2:14–15, Phil.4:8, 1 Pet.3:15, Lk.18:9–14, 1 Pet.5:5, Deut.8:3, Heb.3:1.
9.2.2 2 Cor.4:5, Jn.14:6, Acts 2:39–40, Mic.7:18–19, Acts 4:20.
9.3 **Our Mission and Unbelief**
Psalm 14:1–7, John 20:31, Hebrews 11:6.
9.3.1 Ps.94:3–7, Jn.18:37–8, Ps.115:2.
9.3.2 Judg.6:13, Ex.6:8–9, Ps.73:2–15, 1 Kings 19:1–4, Is.38:18.
9.3.3 Is.63:8–9, Acts 8:32–3, Jn.19:17–20, 1 Jn.4:16–17, Rom.8:22, Acts 20:28, 2 Tim.4:16–18.
9.3.4 Heb.11:35–8, Jer.20:9, Gen.41:14–42, Jn.6:37, 2 Cor.5:17, Mic.6:8, Ps.32:10–11.

Chapter Ten: **OUR HOPE IN GOD**
PSALM 42:1–43:5, LUKE 24:1–52, ROMANS 5:1–5, 1 CORINTHIANS 15:12–58, 2 CORINTHIANS 4:16–5:17, REVELATION 21:1–22:21.

10.1 Is.64:4, Rom.8:18–25, 1 Cor.2:9–10. 2 Pet.3:13, Rev.2:15, Mt.6:10.
10.2 Lk.20:34–6, Lk.1:33, Rev.21:1, Mt.22:1–10, Rev.22:5, Jn.14:2, Rev.21:3, Lk.1:37, Rev.20:14–15.
10.3 2 Cor.5:10, Jn.5:28–9, Mt.25:41, Rom.6:23, 2 Tim.1:8–10, Mt.7:26–7, Ezek.18:20, Rom.9:14–33, Ps.96:11–13, Rom.11:22.
10.4 Jn.11:25–6, Acts 10:40, Jn.6:40, 1 Cor.15:53–4, 1 Jn.5:13, Jn.3:36, Jn.5:24, Gal.3:26–7, Col.2:11–13, Ps.31:5, Lk.23:46.
10.5 Gen.2:7, Rom.11:36, Jn.13:7, Eph.1:9–10, 1 Th.4:16, Mk.13:32–3, 1 Cor.13:12.
10.6 Rev.22:20.
10.7 Rom.15:13.

NOTES

Abbreviations: Geneva Catechism=G.C.; Heidelberg Catechism=H.C.;
Scots Confession=S.C.; Westminster Confession=W.C.;
Westminster Larger Catechism=W.L.C.
Other sources: *A Declaration of Faith*, P.C.U.S.; *Confession of '67*
(U.P.C.U.S.A.); *Our Song of Hope*, Reformed Church in America;
Plan for Union, Joint Commission on Church Union in New Zealand;
Basis for Union, United Reformed Church in the United Kingdom.
With the exception of the latter, where the use is indirect, permission
has been granted for the use of these statements. The style and general
outline for LIVING FAITH follows that of *A Declaration of Faith*.

CHAPTER ONE: GOD

1.1   1–6. S.C., Ch.1; W.C., 11/1 5–6. G.C.Q. 25; **1.2** 1–7. W.C., VII/3–6, 8–10. S.C. Ch.
XII; **1.4** 1–3 G.C.Q. 15; H.C.Q. 22; **1.5** 1–9. G.C.Q. 19; H.C.Q. 25; S.C. Ch.1;
W.C. 11/3; **1.6** 1–3. G.C.Q.7.

CHAPTER TWO: GOD, CREATOR AND RULER

2.1   **God Creates and Rules**
2.1.1 1–7. H.C.Q. 26, 27; W.C., V/1; **2.1.2** 3–6 *A Declaration of Faith* (P.C.U.S.),
Ch. 2/1:8–19; **2.1.3** 1 W.L.C., Q. 7; **2.1.4** 1–6. G.C., Q. 26–29.

2.2   **Our Creation**
2.2.1 1–2. G.C., Q. 2; 5–6. John Calvin, *Institutes*, Bk. I,1,1; 7–9. G.C., Q. 7; H.C.,
Q. 6. W.L.C., Q.1.; **2.2.2** 1–2. W.C., IV/2; *A Declaration of Faith*, Ch. 2/5.

2.3   **Our Calling**
2.3.1 1–3. H.C., Q. 32.

2.4   **Our Care for the World**
2.4.1 1–7. *A Declaration of Faith*, Ch. 2/3:45–60.

2.5   **Sin Separates Us from God**
2.5.1 4–6. S.C.,Ch. 3; W.C., VI/2; **2.5.2** 1–2. G.C., Q. 231–232; H.C., Q. 115. 4–5.
H.C., Q. 113; **2.5.3** 1 W.L.C., Q. 27; 2. W.C., V1/6; 4–5. W.C., V1/2; **2.5.4** 1–7
W.L.C. Q. 28; **2.5.7** 1–2. W.C., IX/3, 3–7. W.C., X1/1–3.

CHAPTER THREE: GOD IN CHRIST

3.1   **Jesus Christ and Israel**
3.1.1 1–5. *A Declaration of Faith*, 3/1:2–5; **3.1.3** 4. *A Declaration of Faith*, Ch. 4/1:7.

3.2   **Jesus Christ: Truly God**
3.2.1 3. D. Bonhoeffer, "Teaching About Christ Begins in Silence", *Christology*
(Collins:Fontana Books, 1975). 6–7. *The Apostles' Creed*, 2nd Article; **3.2.2** 1–4. *The
Nicene Creed*; **3.2.3** 1–2. *The Nicene Creed*, "being of one substance with the Father".

3.3   **Jesus Christ: Truly Human**
3.3.1 1–15. *A Declaration of Faith*, Ch. 4/2:23–48; 9–10. W.C., VIII/3; cf. W.L.C.,

Q. 39. W.L.C., Q. 42.

3.4   **Jesus is Saviour**
3.4.1 1–3. W.C., VIII/1–8. **3.4.2** 3–4. *The Nicene Creed*. "who for us, and for our salvation . . . was made man, and was crucified also for us under Pontius Pilate".; **3.4.3** 1–15. See *Confession of '67* (U.P.C.U.S.A.), 9.09. G.C., Q. 71; H.C., Q. 37.

3.5   **Jesus is Lord**
3.5.1 3–4. G.C., Q. 77–79; H.C., Q. 46–47; W.L.C., Q. 52–53; **3.5.2** 1–4. H.C., Q. 45; W.L.C., Q. 52. 1–2. W.L.C., Q. 54; **3.5.3** 4. H.C., Q. 123; W.L.C., Q. 56; W.C., XXXIII/2–3; **3.5.4** 3. H.C., Q. 31; W.L.C., Q. 44. 3. G.C., Q. 77; H.C., Q. 49; W.L.C., Q. 55.

3.6   **Salvation in Christ**
3.6.1 1–2. H.C., Q. 21; W.L.C., Q. 32. 3–11. S.C., Ch. VIII; W.C., III/5, W.C., X/1; W.L.C., Q. 67; **3.6.2** 8–11. H.C., Q. 1; W.L.C., Q. 79. Regarding 3.6 see General Assembly, *Acts and Proceedings*, 1948, p. 33 and 1970, pp. 290 ff.

CHAPTER FOUR: GOD THE HOLY SPIRIT

4.1   **The Holy Spirit is God with Us**
4.1.1 1–2. H.C., Q. 53; S.C., Ch. XII; W.C. 11/3. 3 *The Nicene Creed*; *A Declaration of Faith*, Ch. 5/1.

4.2   **The Holy Spirit Enables People to Believe**
4.2.1 1–4. W.C., X/2; W.L.C., Q. 58–59. 5–8. *A Declaration of Faith*, Ch. 5/3; 37–42; **4.2.2** 1–8. W.C. XVIII/2–4; W.L.C., Q. 80–81.

CHAPTER FIVE: THE BIBLE

5.1   1–6. W.C., 1/1–4, 7–8. S.C., Ch. XIX; W.C. 1/10; 4–6. *A Declaration of Faith*, Ch. 6/ 3:49–51. 9–12. Preamble and Ordination Questions, *Book of Forms*, 409; W.L.C., Q. 45; **5.2** 1–2. W.C., 1/5; 4–6. *A Declaration of Faith*, Ch. 6/3:55–6; 8–9. *A Declaration of Faith*, Ch. 6/3:46–8; **5.4** 3–6. W.C., 1/8; 7–12. S.C., Ch. XVIII; W.C. 1/6–7, *Confession of '67*, 9.27–30.

CHAPTER SIX: FAITH

6.1   **Faith**
6.1.1 1–2. "Basis of Union", The United Reformed Church in the United Kingdom, 12; H.C., Q. 65; W.C., XIV/1. 4–9. H.C., Q. 21; W.C., XIV/2; W.L.C., Q. 72; **6.2.1** 1–11. W.C. XIV/3; **6.2.3** 1–5. W.C. XIV/3; W.L.C. Q. 80. cf. W.C. XVIII/4.

CHAPTER SEVEN: GOD'S CHURCH

7.1   **The Church**
7.1.2 1–3. "Plan for Union", Joint Commission on Church Union in New Zealand, Sec. 5; **7.1.3** 1–3. G.C., Q. 96; **7.1.4** 1–3. G.C., Q. 97; H.C., Q. 54; S.C., Ch. XVI; **7.1.6** 1–8. W.C., XXV/4–5.

7.2   **Ministry**
7.2.1 1. "Basis of Union", United Reformed Church in the United Kingdom, Sec. 19;

7.2.3 1–9. G.C., Q. 306–307; W.C., XXV/3; "Pastors", *The Form of Presbyterial Church Government*; **7.2.4** 1–5. "Other Church Governors", *The Form of Presbyterial Church Government*; **7.2.5** 1–5. "Teacher or Doctor", *The Form of Presbyterial Church Government*.

7.3   Worship
7.3.3 1–5. H.C., Q. 32.

7.4   Preaching
7.4.1 1–11. *Confession of '67*, 9.21–26; H.C., Q. 84; **7.4.2** 1–5. "Of the Preaching of the Word", *The Westminster Directory for the Public Worship of God.*

7.5   Sacraments
7.5.1 1–2. S.C., Ch. XXI; W.C., XXVII/1. 3–5. H.C., Q. 66; **7.5.2** 1–2. W.C. XXVII/2; **7.5.3** 1–5. W.C., XXVII/3.

7.6   Baptism
7.6.1 1–2. H.C., Q. 69; W.C., XXVII/1; **7.6.2** 1–4. W.C., XXVIII/2. 5–7 Adapted from the *Book of Common Order* 1979, Church of Scotland, p. 47 cf. H.C., Q. 73; **7.6.3** 1–2. W.C., XXVIII/6; 5–7 W.L.C., Q. 167; 8–11. H.C., Q. 74; W.C., XXVIII/ 4; **7.6.4** 3–4. H.J. Wotherspoon and J.M. Kirkpatrick, *A Manual of Church Doctrine according to the Church of Scotland* (London: Oxford Press 1960), Revised and enlarged by T.F. Torrance and Ronald Selby Wright, p. 23.; **7.6.5** 1. W.C., XXVIII/1; 2–4 H.C., Q.1; 7–8 Wotherspoon and Kirkpatrick, p. 23.

7.7   Holy Communion
7.7.1 1–2. H.C., Q. 75; W.C. XXIX/1; **7.7.2** 1–2. "Our Song of Hope", Reformed Church in America, 19. 3–6. H.C., Q. 79; S.C., Ch. XXI; W.C., XXIX/1 and 7; **7.7.3** 1–5. H.C., Q. 75. 6–8. "Our Song of Hope", 19; **7.7.4** 6–9. W.C., XXVIII/1.

CHAPTER EIGHT: OUR LIFE IN CHRIST

8.1   Discipleship
8.1.2 and 3 1–5. H.C., Q. 55; W.C., XXVI/1; *Confession of '67*, 9.22–23; **8.1.4** 1–3. H.C., Q. 116–117; W.L.C., Q. 178; 7–9. G.C., Q. 244; G.C., Q. 252; **8.1.6** 1–4. H.C., Q. 103. See *Acts and Proceedings*, 1966, pp. 238–239.

8.2   The Christian Family
8.2.5 1–4. *A Declaration of Faith*, Ch. 2/5:106–109; **8.2.6** 1–7. H.C., Q. 55.

8.3   Love
8.3.1 1. Adapted from Ian Cowie, *People Praying* (Edinburgh: St. Andrew Press, 1972), p. 67. 5. *Ibid.*

8.4   Justice
8.4.1 H.C., Q. 123; *A Declaration of Faith*, Ch. 8/5, esp. 64–66, 70–72, 77–78.

8.5   World Peace
8.5.3 6. *A Declaration of Faith*, Ch. 8/5.

CHAPTER NINE: THE CHURCH REACHES OUT

9.1   Our Mission
9.1.1 1. W.L.C., Q. 191.

CHAPTER TEN: OUR HOPE IN GOD

10.1   5–6. H.C., Q. 123; W.L.C., Q. 191; **10.2** 1. *Confession of '67*, 9.53–56; **10.3** 6–7. W.L.C., Q. 60; **10.4** 1–11. H.C., Q. 57–58; W.L.C., Q. 86; **10.5** 8–9. W.L.C., Q. 90.